Trees

Julie Murray

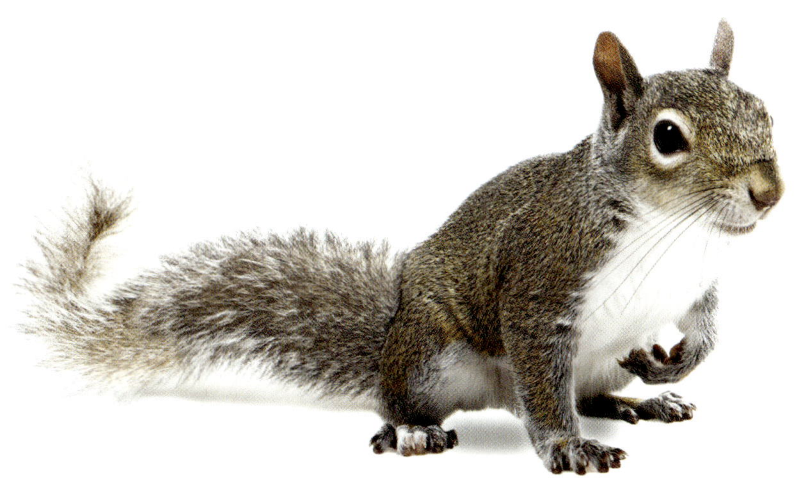

Abdo Kids Junior
is an Imprint of Abdo Kids
abdobooks.com

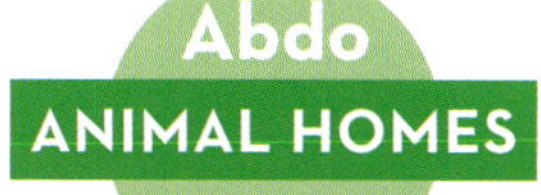

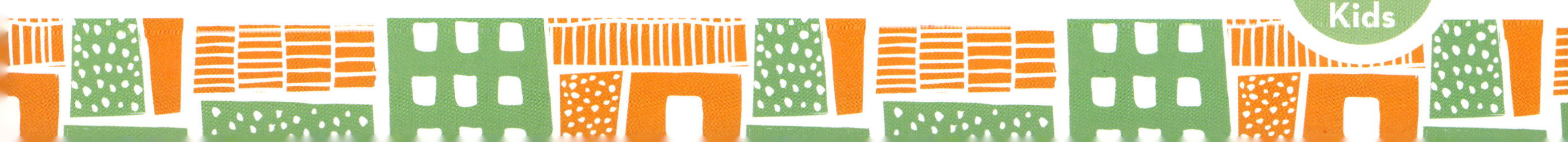

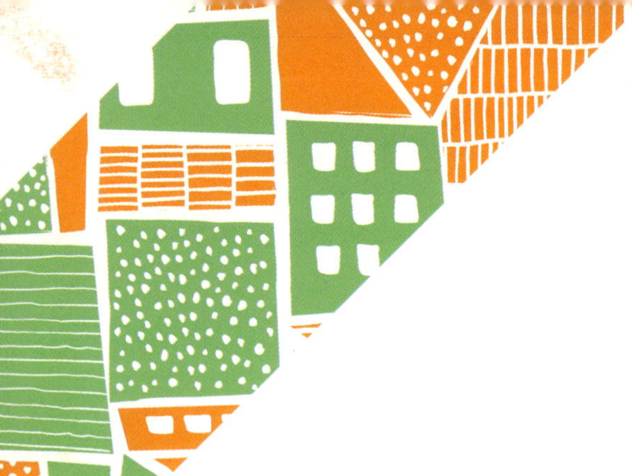

abdobooks.com

Published by Abdo Kids, a division of ABDO, P.O. Box 398166, Minneapolis, Minnesota 55439.

Printed in the United States of America, North Mankato, Minnesota.

052019

092019

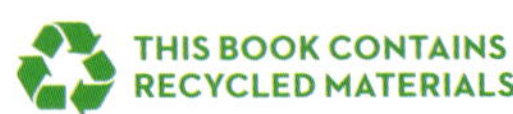

Photo Credits: Alamy, iStock, Shutterstock

Production Contributors: Teddy Borth, Jennie Forsberg, Grace Hansen

Design Contributors: Christina Doffing, Candice Keimig, Dorothy Toth

Library of Congress Control Number: 2018963576

Publisher's Cataloging-in-Publication Data

Names: Murray, Julie, author.

Title: Trees / by Julie Murray.

Description: Minneapolis, Minnesota : Abdo Kids, 2020 | Series: Animal homes | Includes online resources and index.

Identifiers: ISBN 9781532185250 (lib. bdg.) | ISBN 9781644941225 (pbk.) | ISBN 9781532186233 (ebook) | ISBN 9781532186721 (Read-to-me ebook)

Subjects: LCSH: Animal housing--Juvenile literature. | Tree-dwellings--Juvenile literature. | Woodlands--Juvenile literature. | Animals--Habitations--Juvenile literature.

Classification: DDC 591.564--dc23

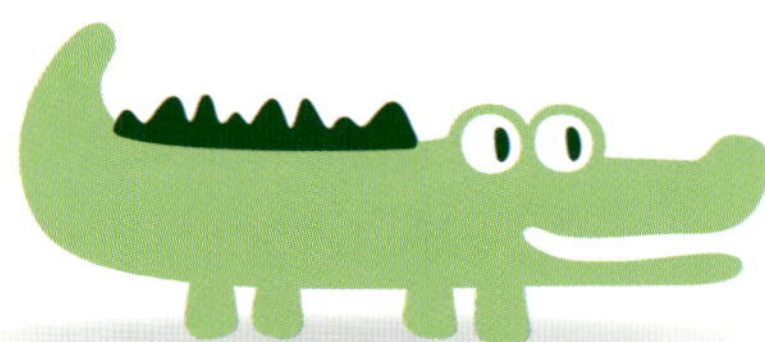

Table of Contents

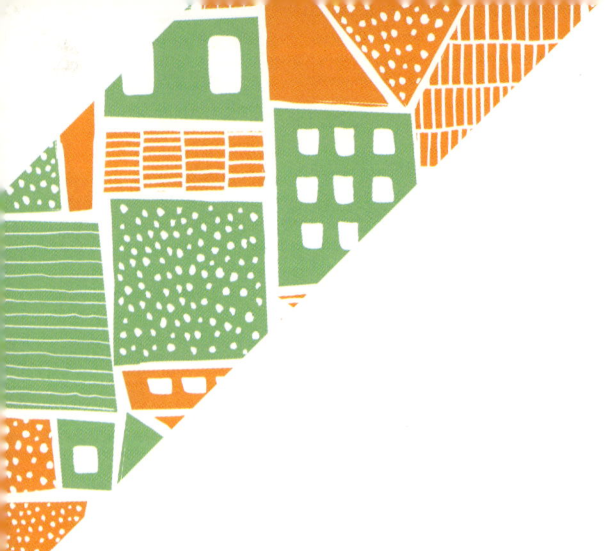

Trees

Many kinds of animals live in trees.

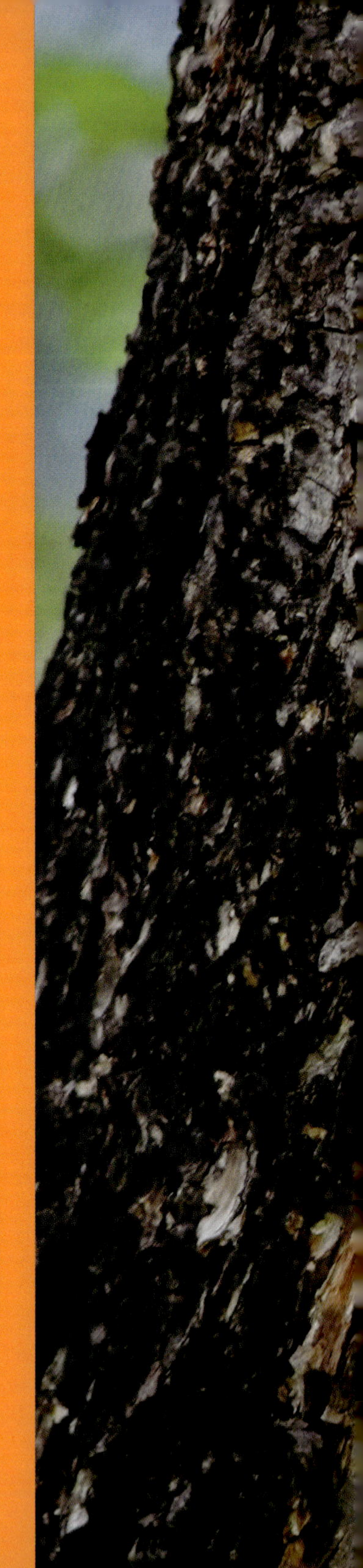

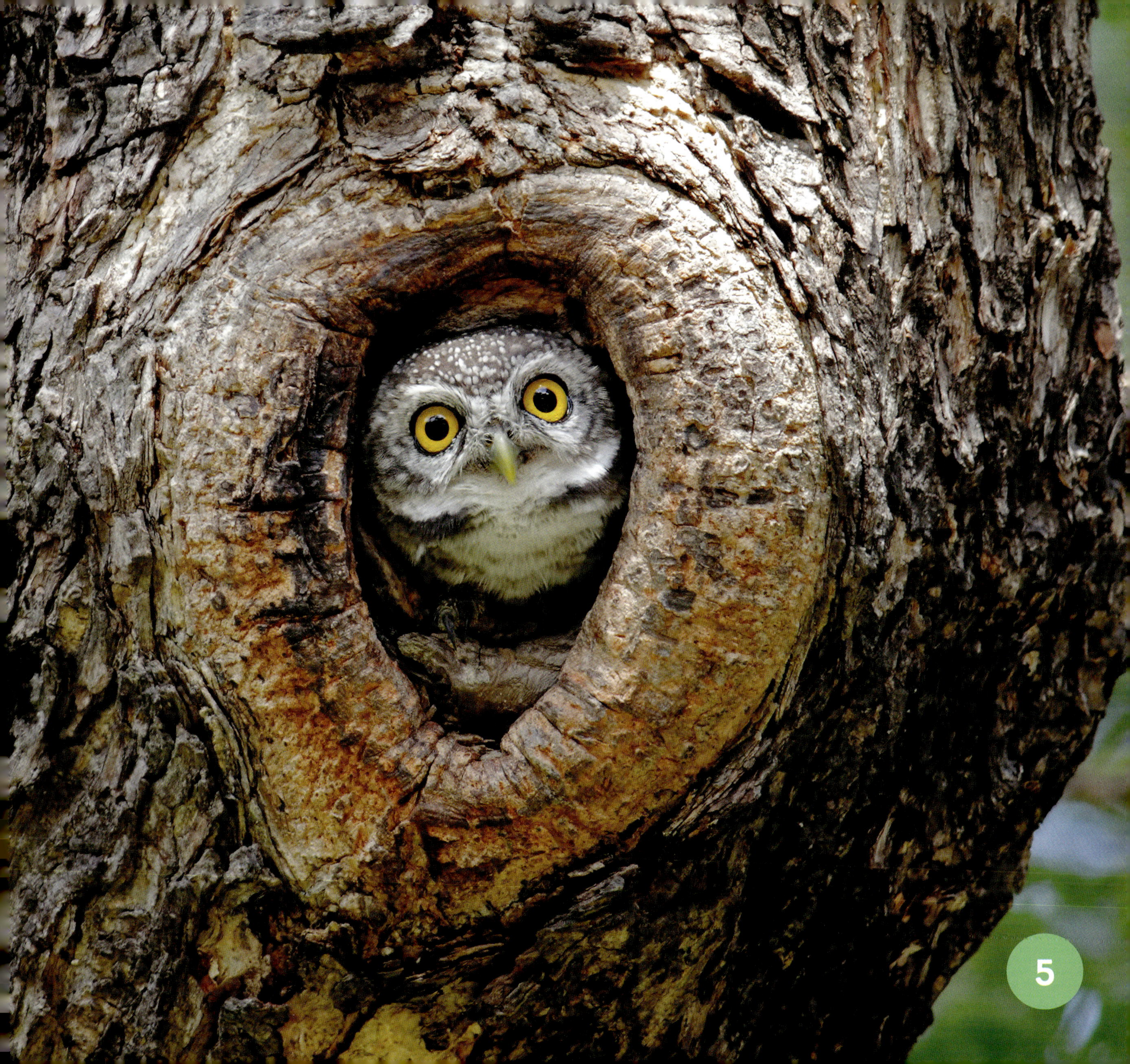

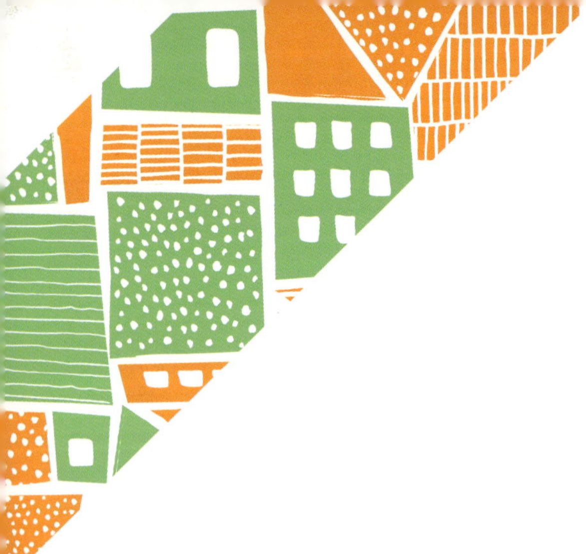

Birds make nests in trees. This is where they lay their eggs.

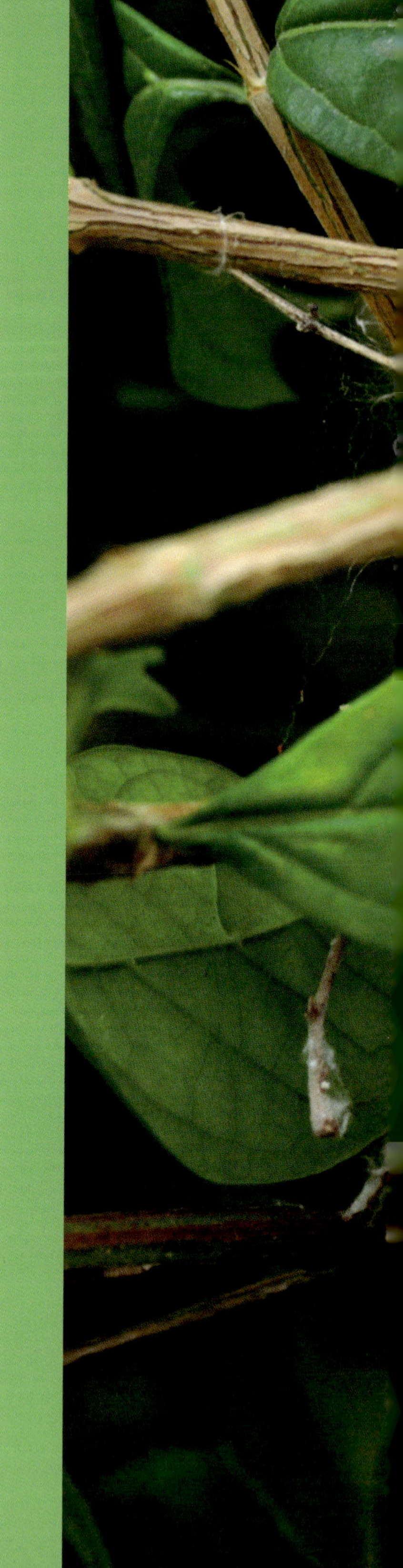

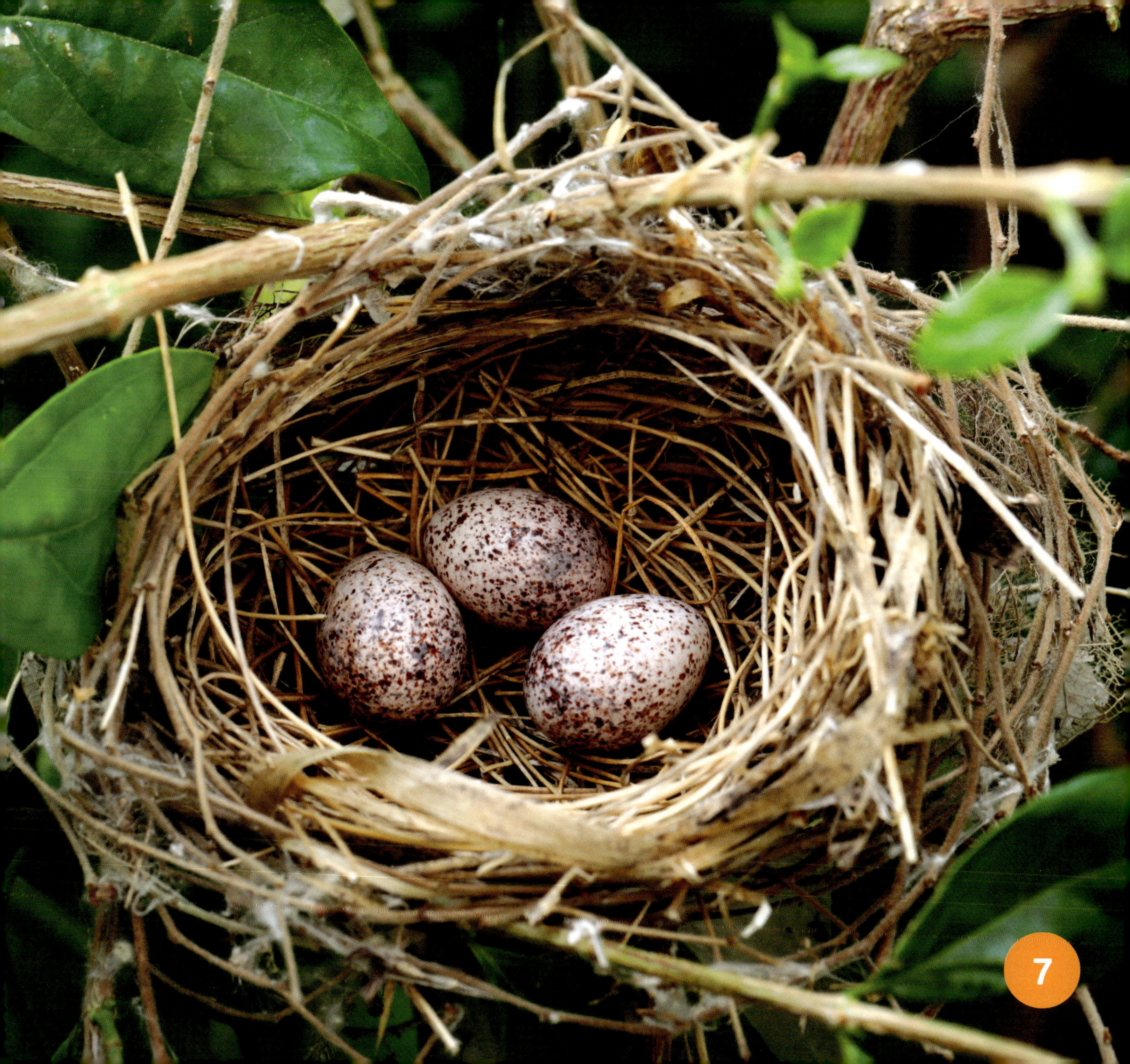

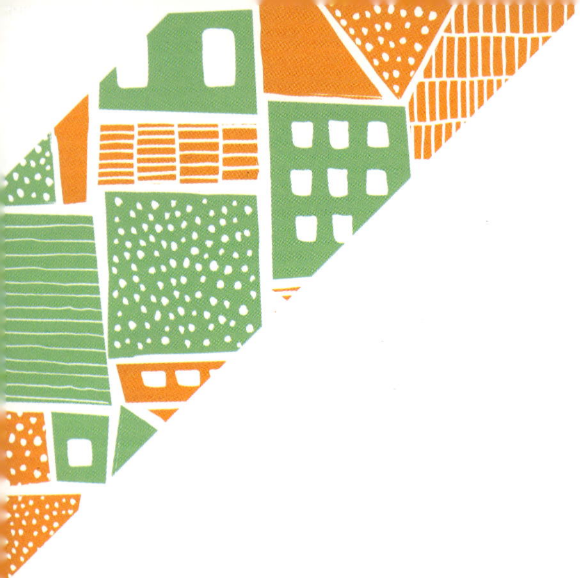

Squirrels live in trees. They **collect** nuts for the winter.

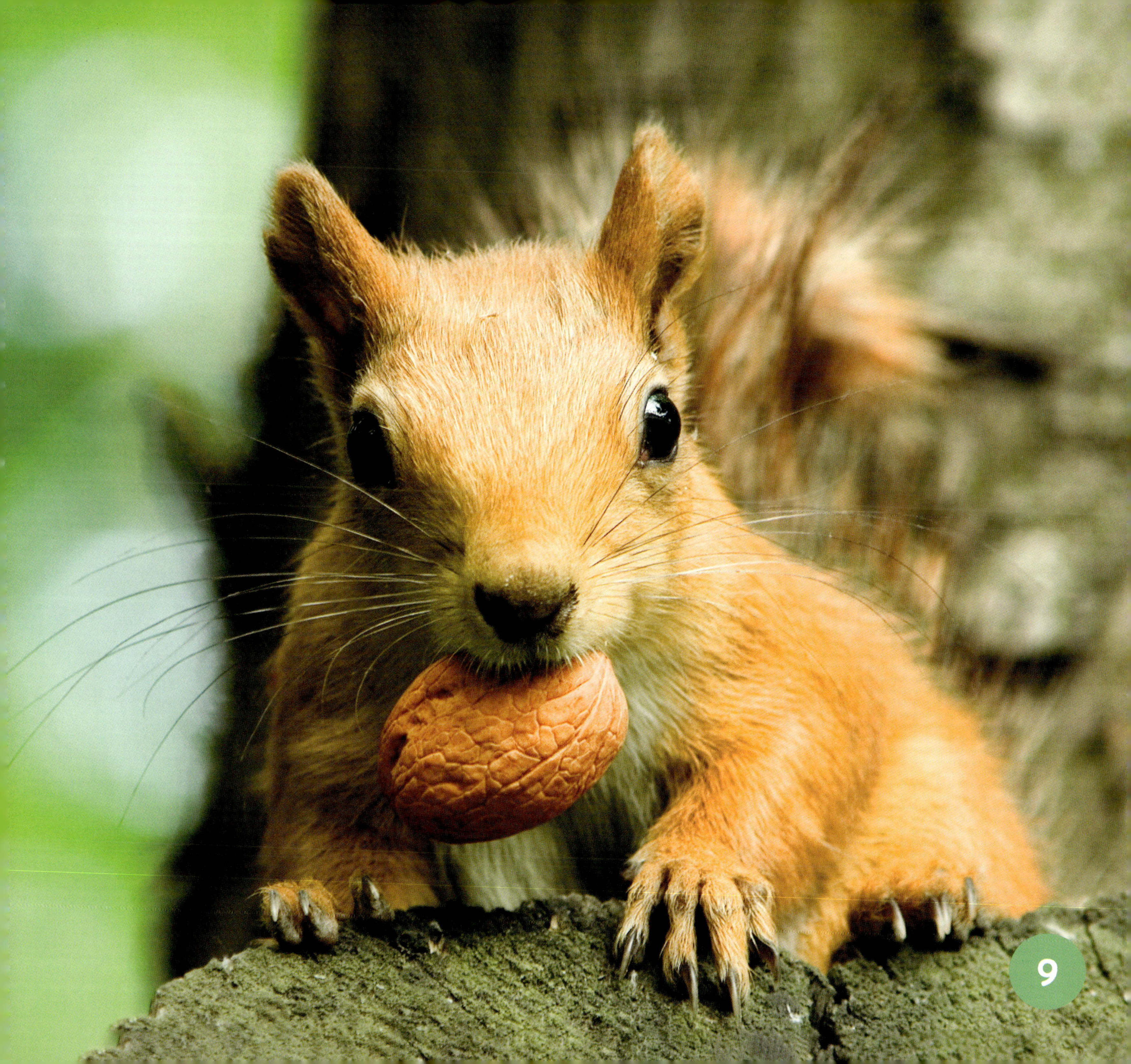

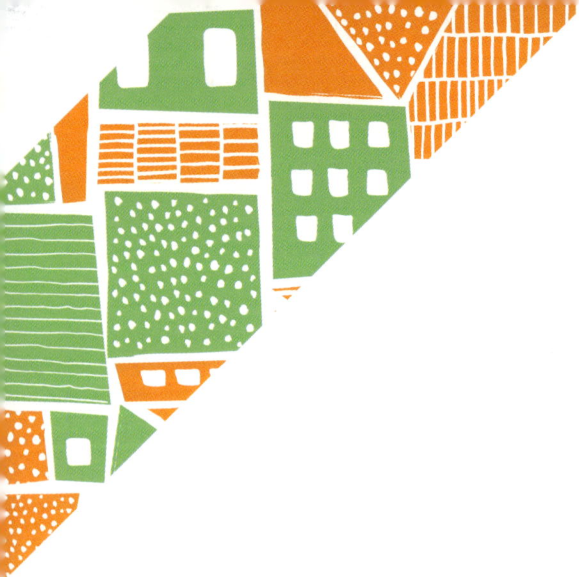

Some owls live in trees.

They sleep all day.

They hunt at night.

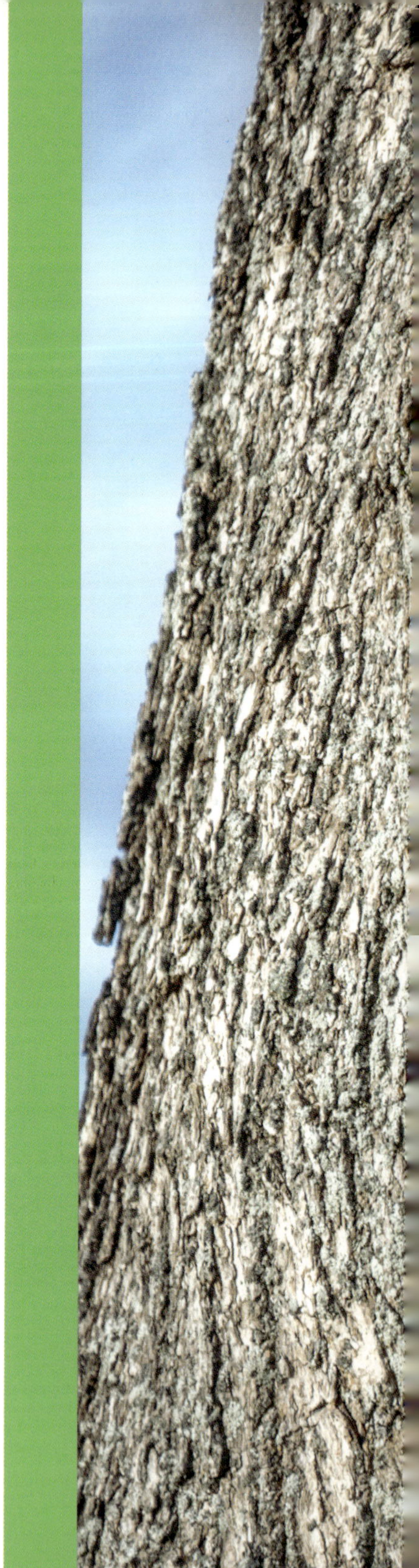

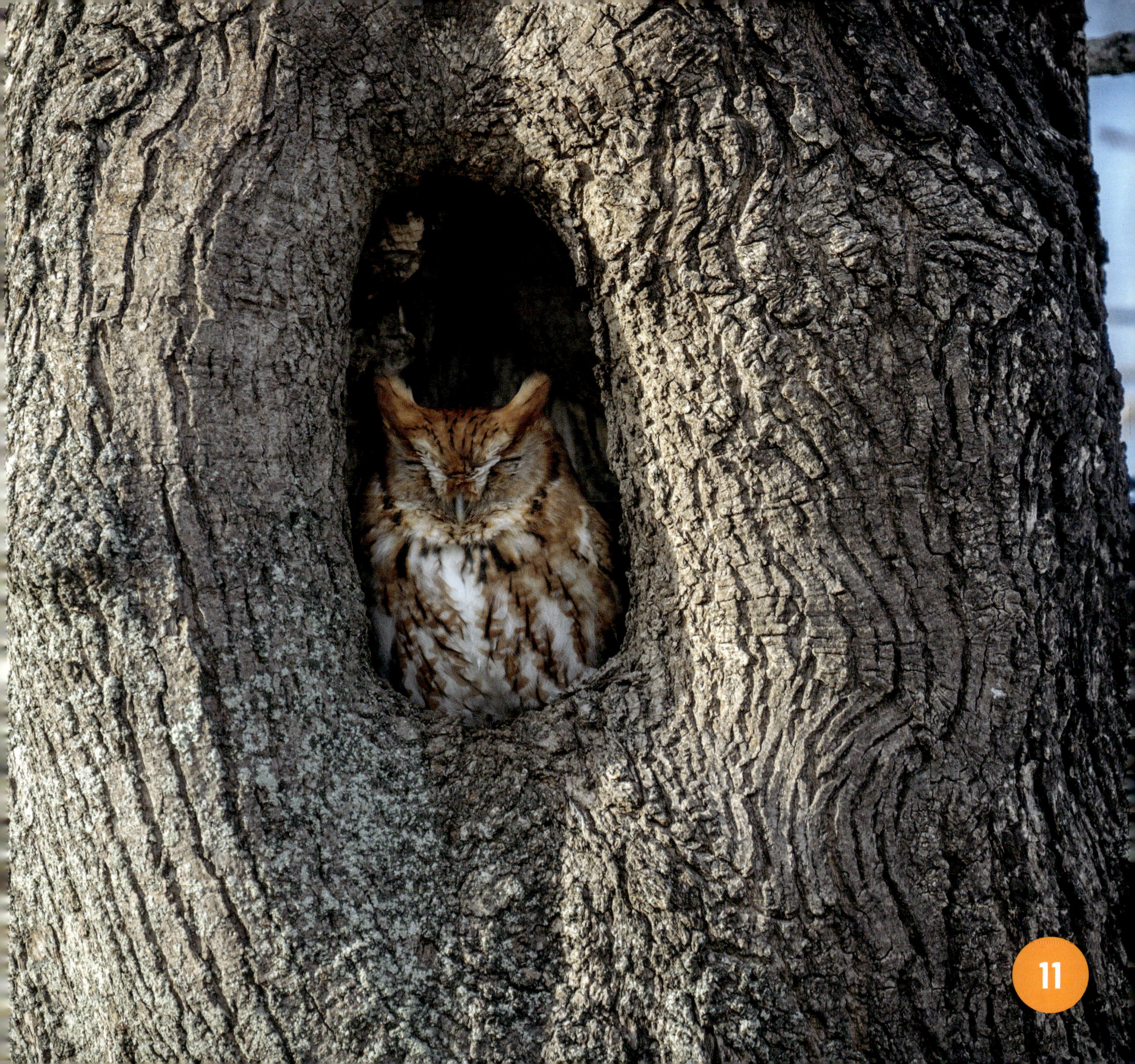

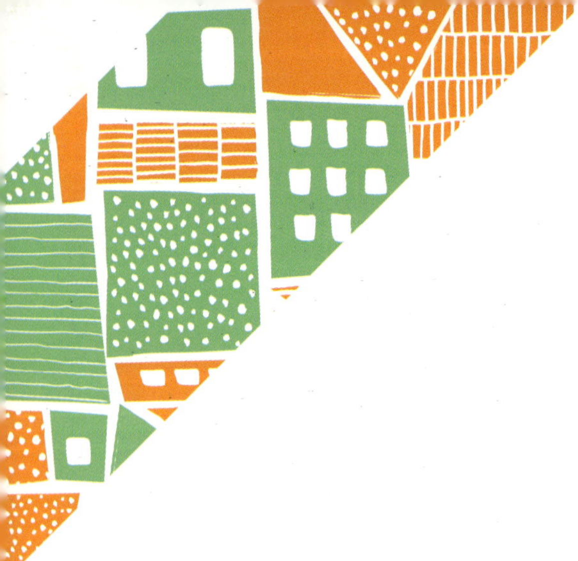

Honey bees live in trees. Their hive hangs from a **branch**.

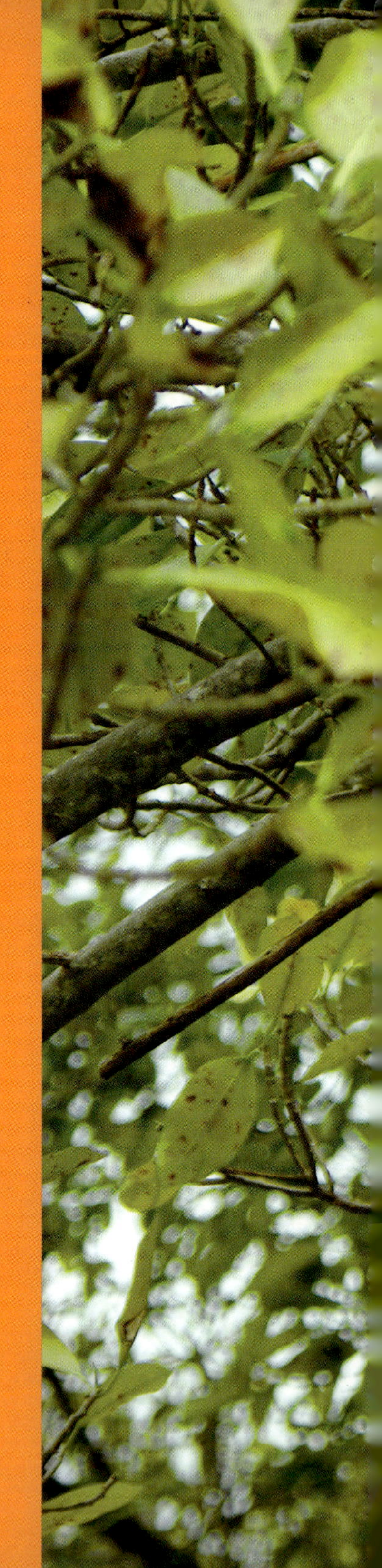

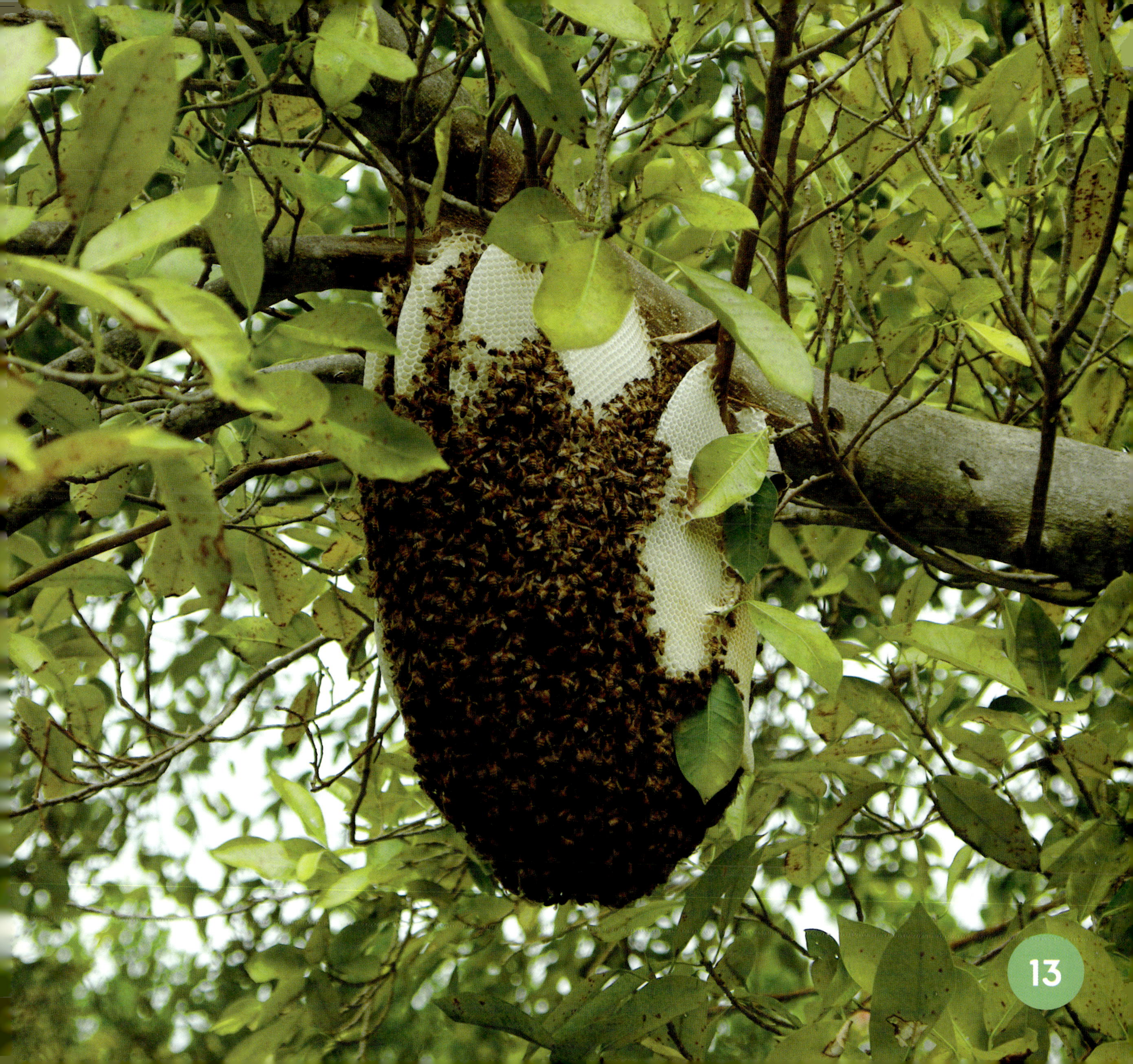

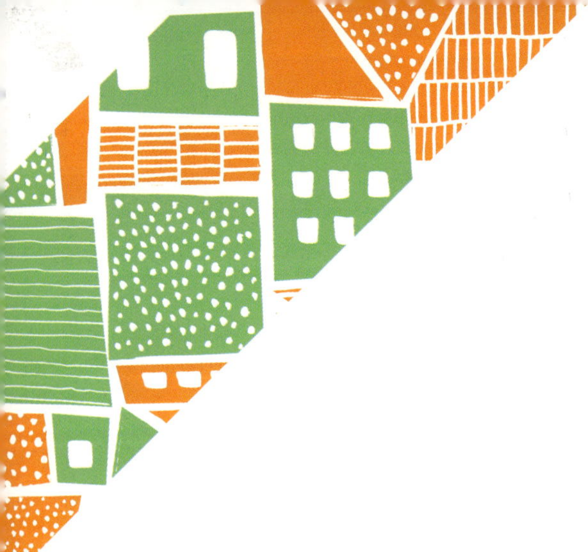

Some frogs live in trees. A tree frog can jump 7 feet (2.1 m)!

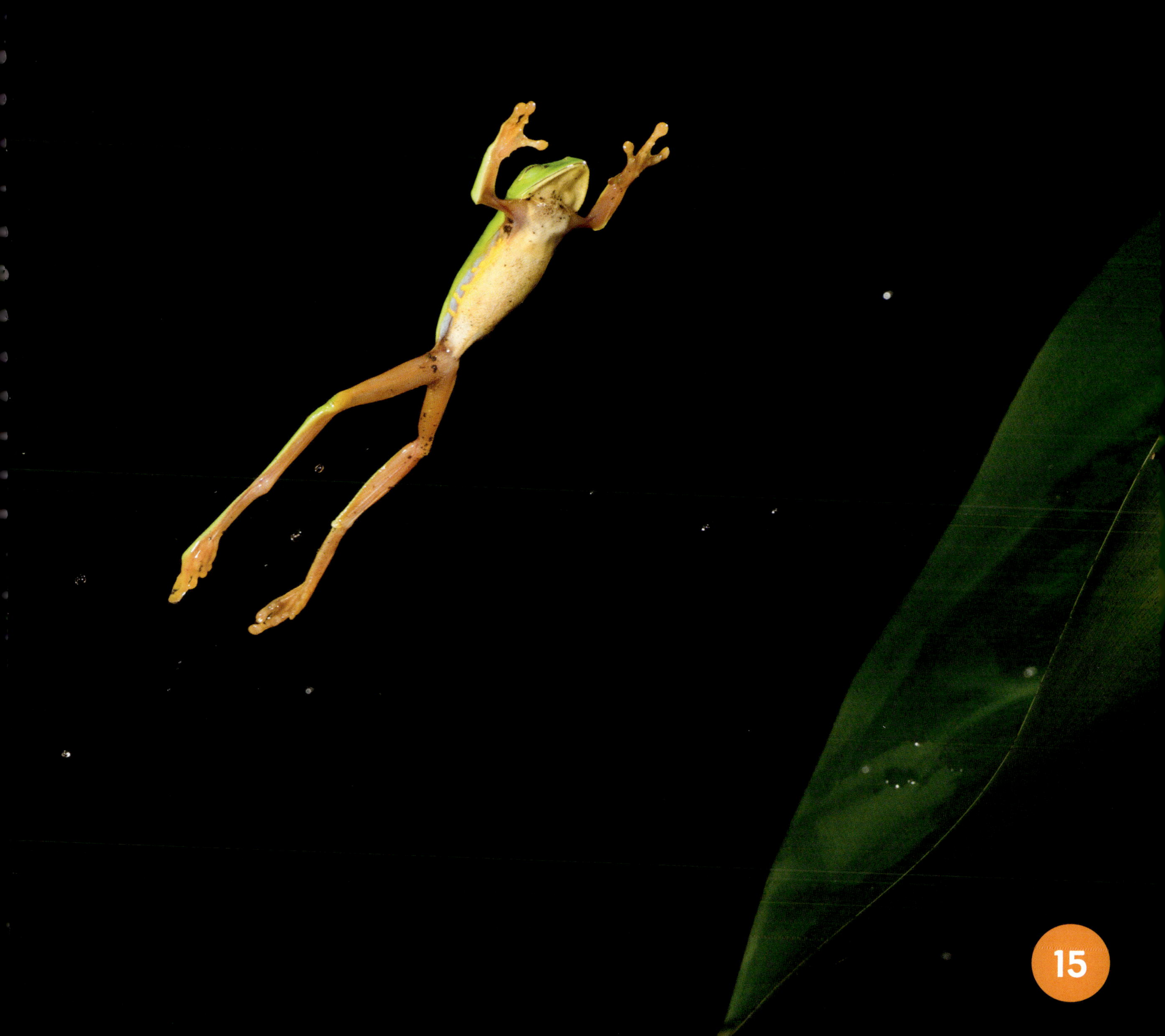

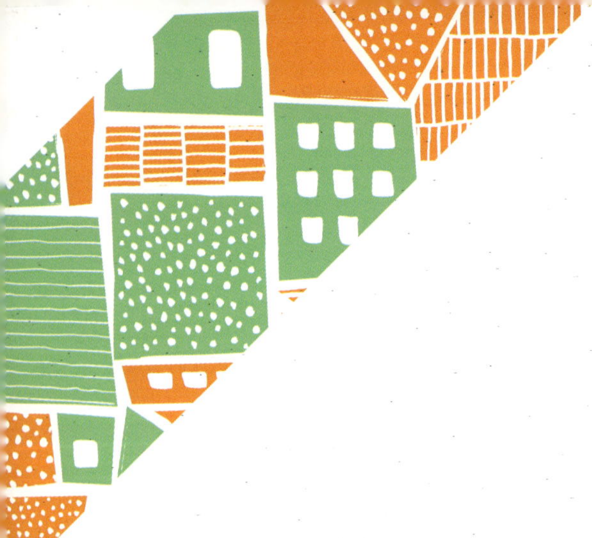

Some monkeys live in trees.

Howler monkeys sit high up.

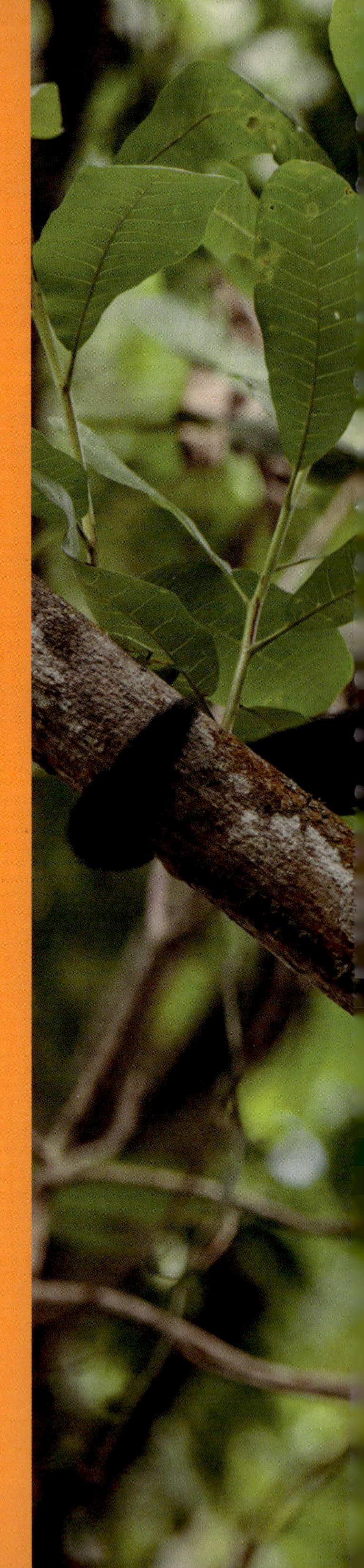

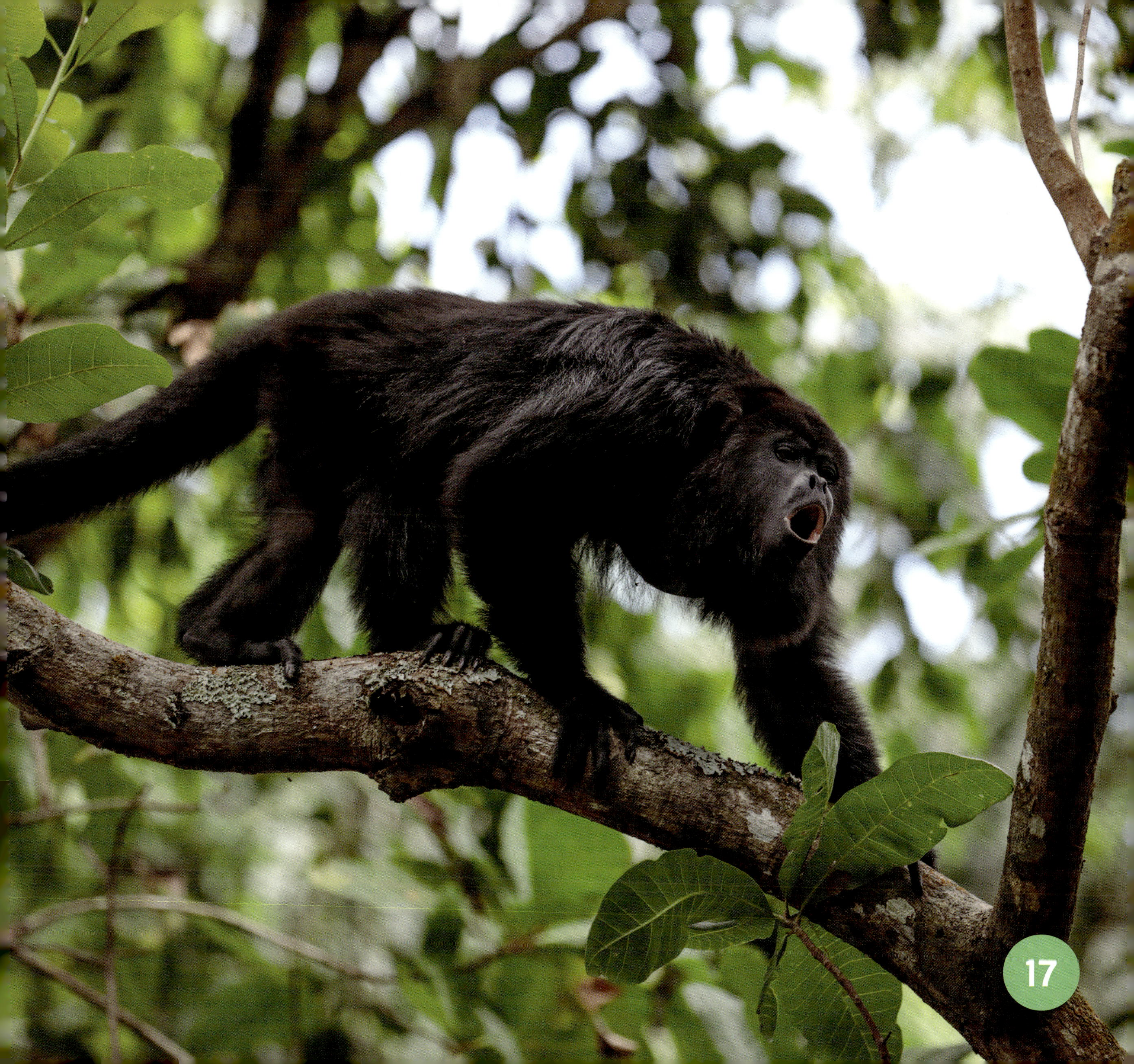

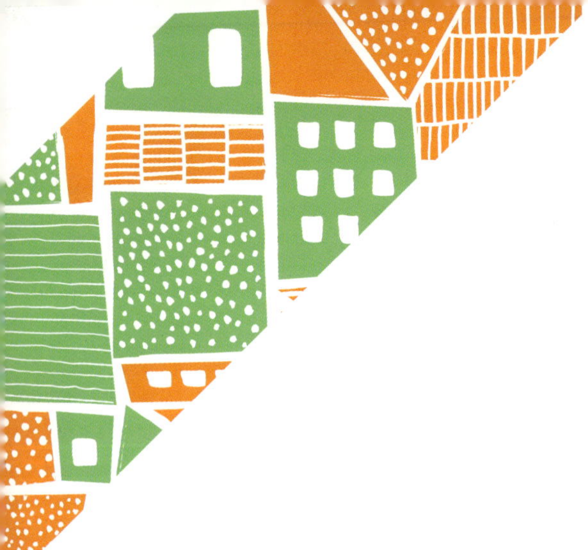

Koalas live in **eucalyptus trees**.

They only eat the tree's leaves.

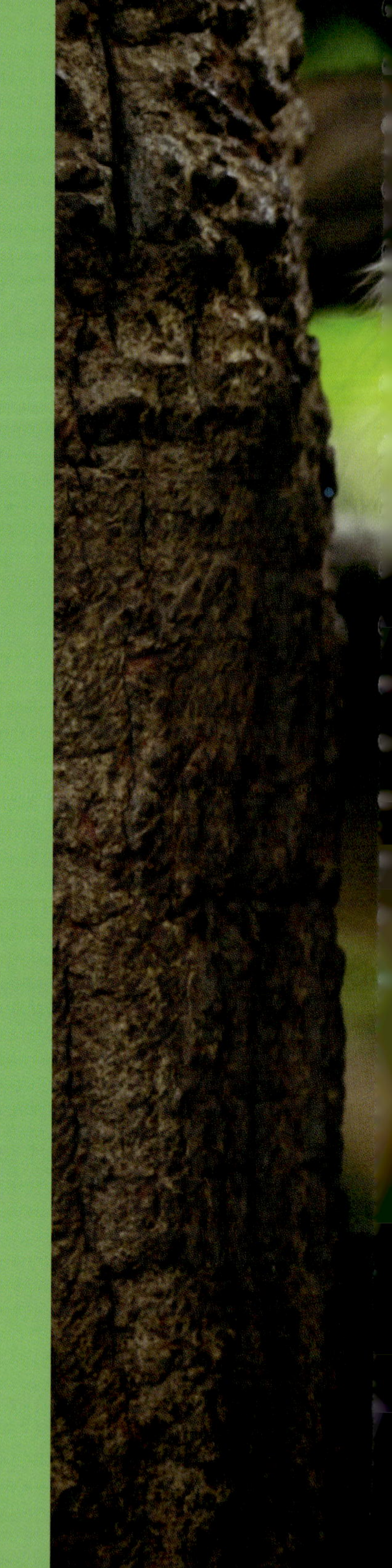

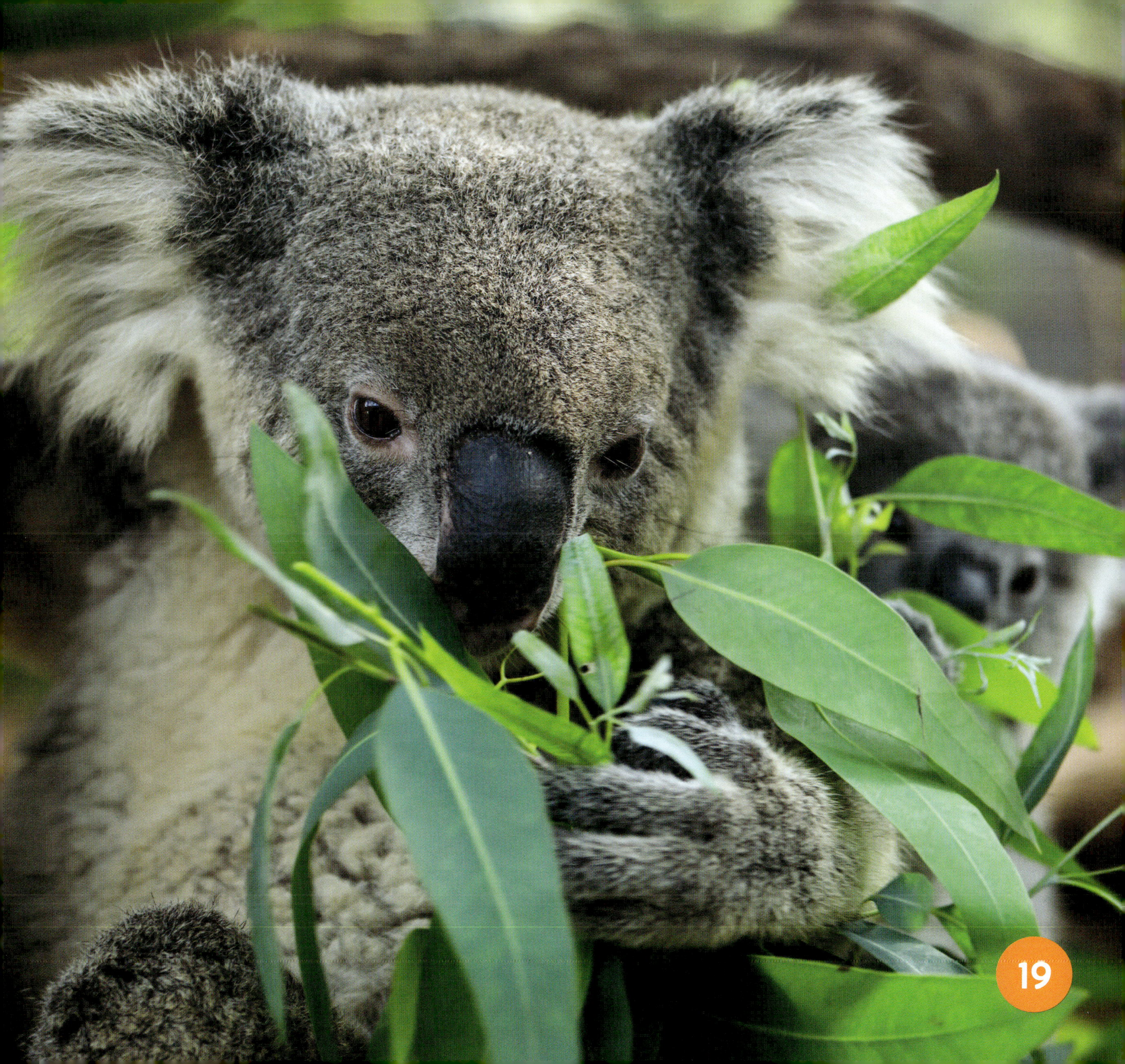

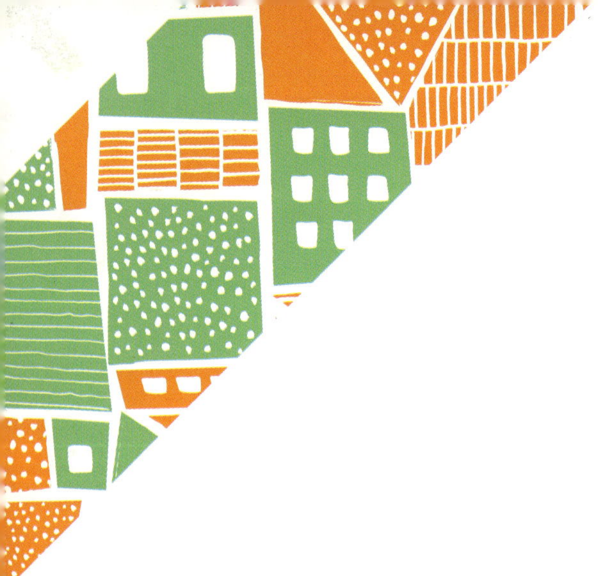

What have you seen living in a tree?

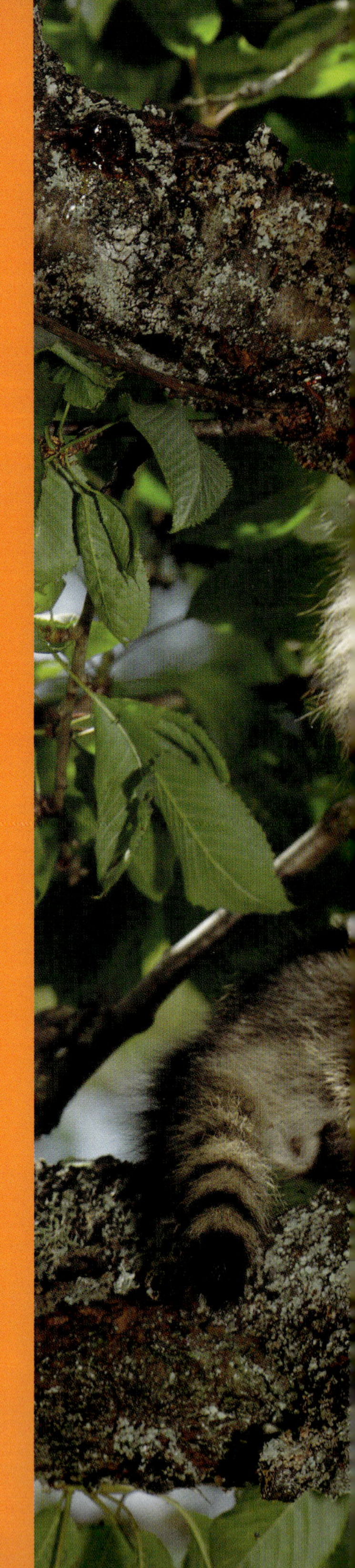

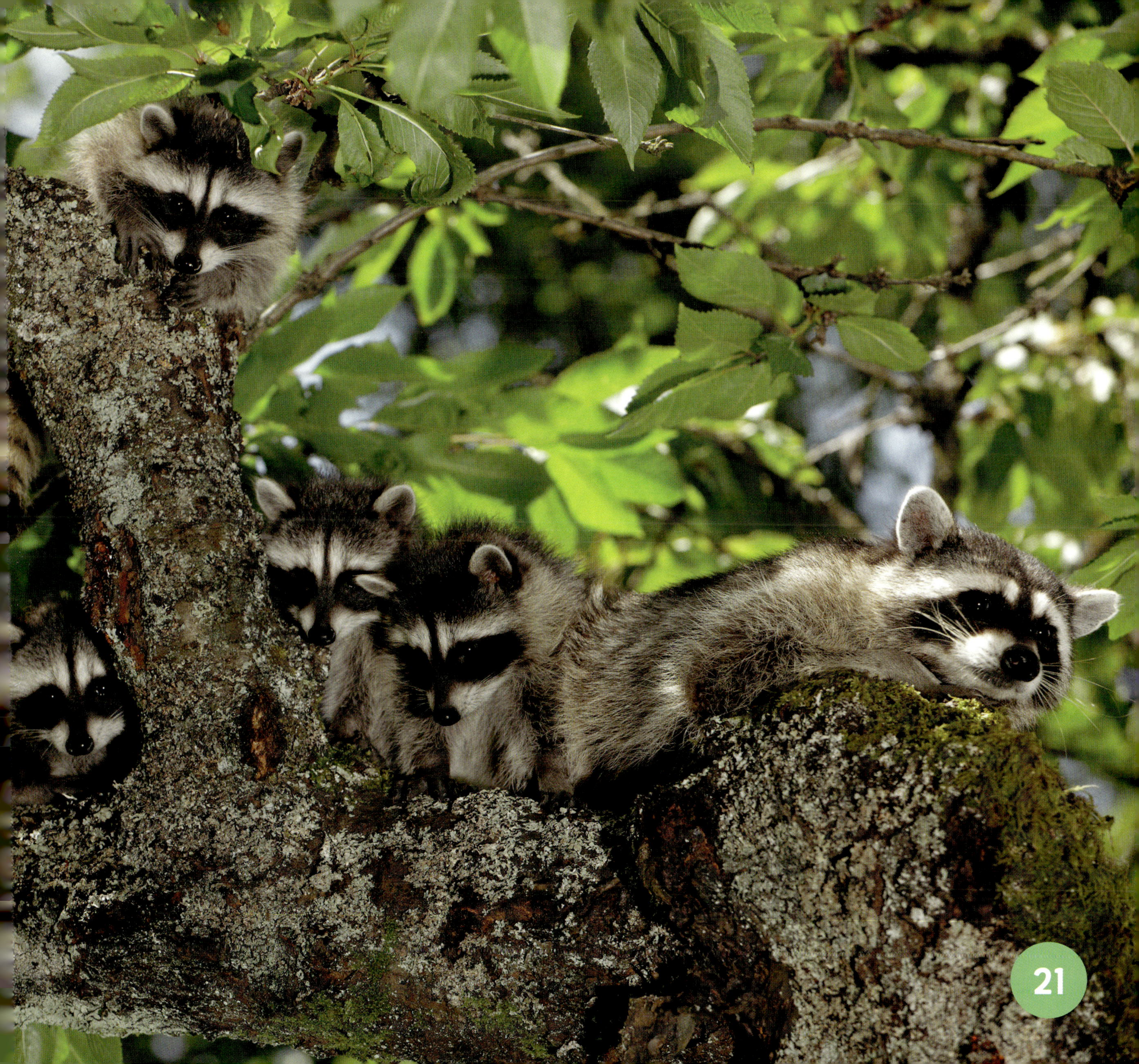

What Lives in a Tree?

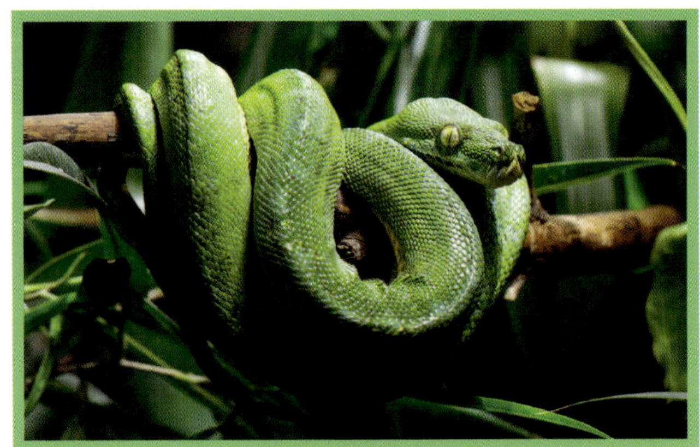

green tree pythons

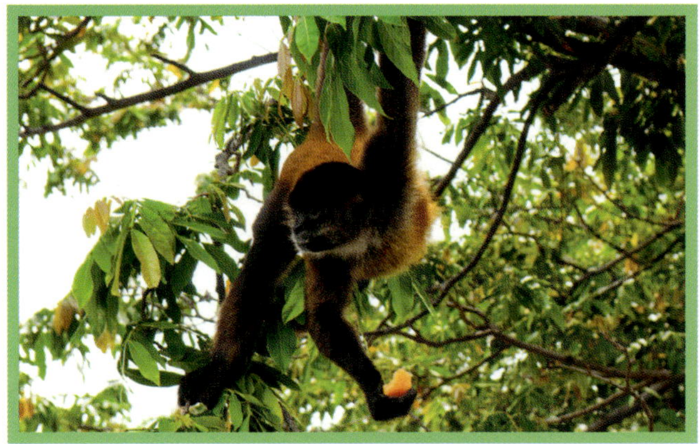

spider monkeys

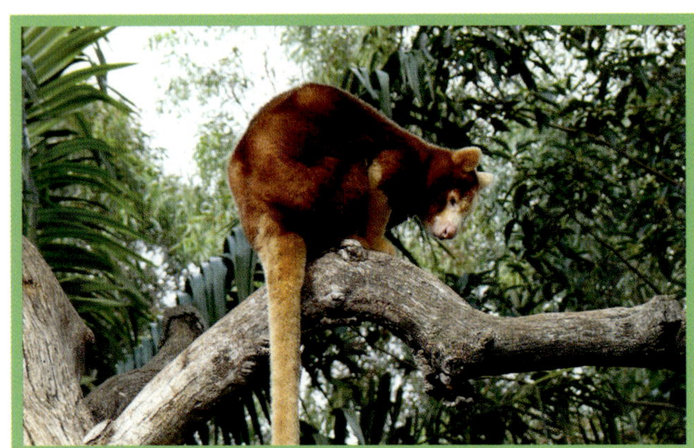

tree kangaroos

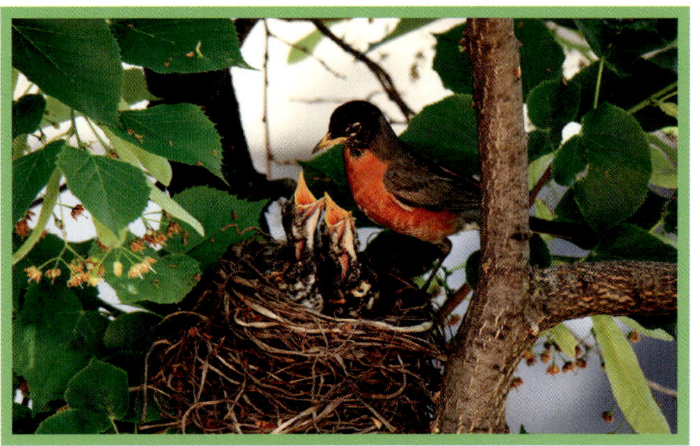

robins

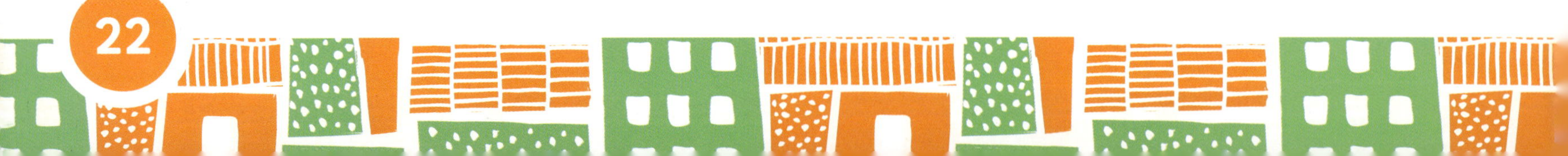

Glossary

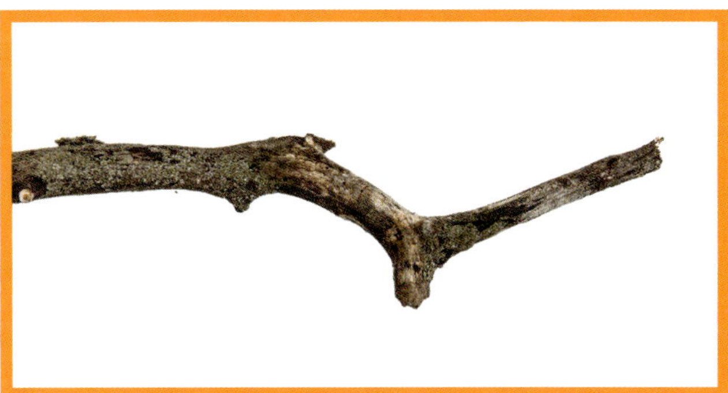

branch
a woody part of a tree that grows out from the trunk.

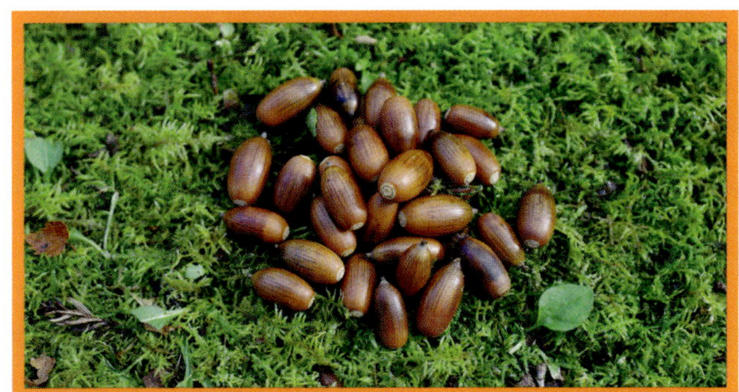

collect
to gather together.

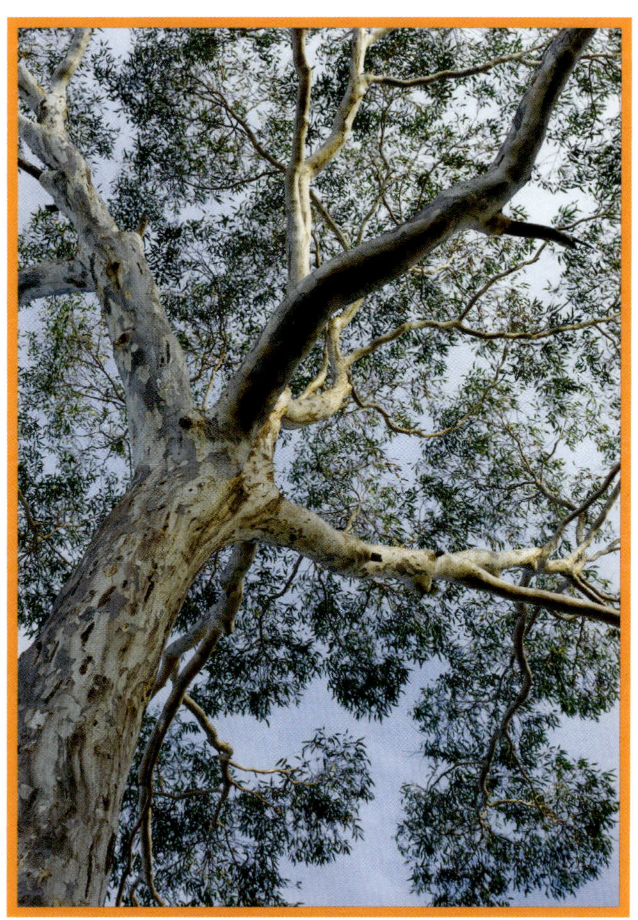

eucalyptus tree
a kind of tall evergreen tree native to Australia.

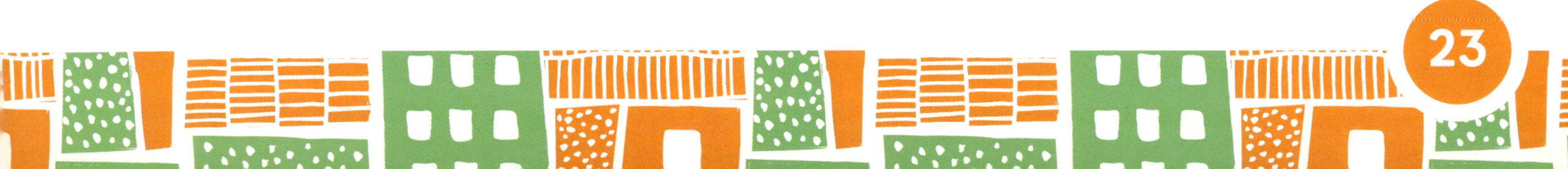

Index

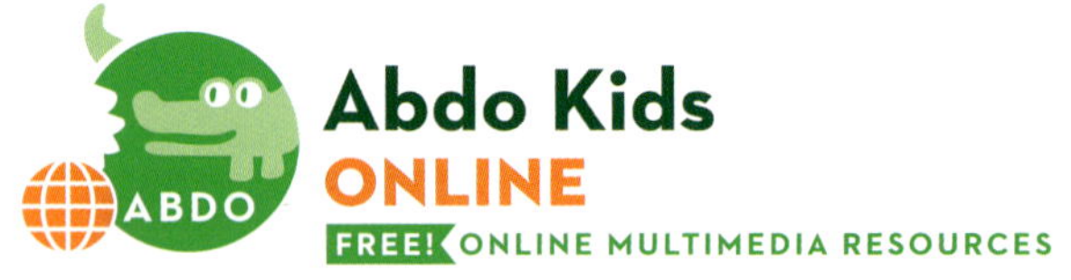

Visit **abdokids.com**

to access crafts, games,

videos, and more!

Use Abdo Kids code

ATK5250

or scan this QR code!

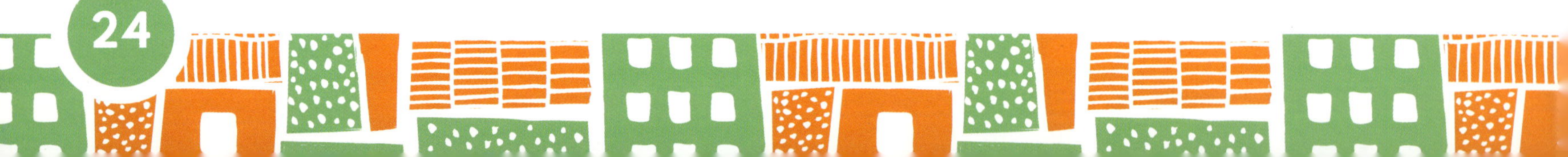